MW00997997
DERWENT • WATERCOLOUR
Turquoise Blue 39
CARAN d'ACHE
SUPRACOLOR II Soft
PRISMACOLOR | PREMIER
LIGHT AQUA
BLEU-VERT PÂLE
Luminance 6901
KOBALTTÜRKIS HELL LIGHT COBALT TURQUOISE
Albrecht Dürer
FABER-CASTELL
BLEU TURQUOISE
VERT TURQUOISE
CARAN d'ACHE · SWISS MADE
GERMANY

WINDOWS
at TIFFANY & CO.

Slipcase cover: Tiffany High Impact, Fall, 2017. Photo © Ricky Zehavi.
Endpages: © Dan Wonderly.

3 Park Avenue, 27th Floor
New York, NY 10016 USA
Tel: 212-989-6769 Fax: 212-647-0005
www.assouline.com
Editorial director: Esther Kremer
Art director: Jihyun Kim
Editor: Justin O'Neill
Photo editor: Hannah Hayden
Printed in China.
ISBN: 9781614287490

WINDOWS
at TIFFANY & Co.

ASSOULINE

TIFFANY & CO.
727

In the beginning, there was the showman. Charles Lewis Tiffany, it should be noted, was a contemporary of P.T. Barnum, and his willingness to be outrageous, inventive, and seductive, all in the name of drawing crowds, was a trait he shared with the creator of "The Greatest Show on Earth." He understood, long before his time, the desire people had to see things they had never experienced and the basic human hunger to dream about something bigger than one's self. He fed this hunger in his windows, from his very first store in New York City.

Back on the Bowery in the 1800s, penny arcades drew in New Yorkers from all walks of life to spend money and be entertained in a democratic, pedestrian way. At the time, New York was so much about museums behind glass, about inaccessibility and exclusion. But there are references in a novel from the 1800s about the windows at Tiffany being "on fire with diamonds," lovely visions that people were drawn to like moths to a flame. It was a destination, public theater, vivid spectacle, all-inclusive,

The façade of Tiffany's flagship store. Photo © Andrew Bordwin.

and completely unprecedented. And because Charles Lewis Tiffany understood the importance of theatricality in window display, he was willing to put everything, including the kitchen sink, in his windows, if that's what it took to pull a crowd.

•

In the early days, Tiffany's windows were bursting with objects, a virtual riot of product and aspiration. In an archival photograph from the flagship in 1876 located at 15 Union Square West, the windows are voluptuously draped in fabric with objects and treasures pinned on, a million nude statues, jewelry and pearls scattered about and, because why not add some more icing to the icing, fake flowers. A little guardrail was installed up against the glass where one could rest one's gloved hands and parasol, inviting a stop to stare and study. This was very much the purpose of a window display—to set a stage and allow the public to dream about the treasure and possibility the world holds. This thoughtful orchestration allowed every man, woman, and child on the street to stop and get lost in a dream. This is what windows do. They allow a view into a literal store, but farther and deeper into a fantasy, into another world. For Charles Lewis Tiffany, windows were never a secondary communication tool. They were always an opportunity to express something far greater than what one could possibly ever talk about.

Tiffany's windows were large then, so multiple people could line up in front of them, as one would at a natural history museum, except in this case, one actually became part of the scene, and the world created before your eyes actually become your life. People who do windows understand that they are creating memories for people, that they are sending them off gently, or sometimes abruptly, into dreams. The viewer finds himself in a completely constructed world, a concept that no one had considered before Tiffany. Their windows were like a public museum, but one that anyone could participate in. The purpose was to entertain, to surprise, to express something larger. And, of course, to create desire.

By the time Gene Moore entered the scene in 1955, after the company's next creative director, Louis Comfort Tiffany, had passed away, the world of the windows took another turn. Moore was brought to Tiffany from Bonwit Teller by the company's former chairman Walter Hoving. Moore was well known at Bonwit Teller for creating extremely theatrical scenes, and was charged by Hoving with designing great windows that were fashionable, in good taste, and that spoke to what was current. He was also, in an unprecedented show of trust, given complete carte blanche to create whatever he felt.

His windows were in touch with the times, topical and occasionally outrageous. If there were an art gallery with something fabulous going on, that would turn up in Moore's windows. If there were a retrospective at the Metropolitan Museum of Art, Moore would make make a nod to it in his displays. If he knew the Easter parade was happening the next week, he would plant grass in the windows so that New Yorkers parading their extravagant bonnets on Fifth Avenue would come by and see the lush spectacle. His work inevitably tied back to what was happening culturally. If there was a water restriction in the city or taxes were due, he would comment on that. Always, there was a localized connection from the concept to execution, so that the window had a tongue-in-cheek finger on the pulse and anyone could relate.

Gene Moore reigned on Fifth Avenue and defined window display as we know it today. He understood the importance of telling a story, yet he was able to mesmerize people with visions created from the most humble, raw, and uncomplicated materials. He lined the windows with felt and burlap, and used household string, bobbins, pasta, gumdrops, and popcorn. He had an aesthetic that was simple and handmade, but with an artistic sensibility that elevated every scene, creating the divine from the ordinary, unafraid to mix the mundane with the magnificent.

In one famous window, he piled a toy dump truck with sand and nestled an enormous diamond in the midst, creating a tension between materials that gave the gemstone a nobility even more brilliant than if it had been laid out on the finest velvet. In another, a bird pulled a diamond necklace from the earth like a worm. He was unafraid to use humor, juxtaposition, and ambiguity to take the seriousness out of seriously expensive jewelry and create worlds that anyone could participate in. And he lit every scenario himself, simply, cleanly, and very often with a favorite signature blue filter that was soon named Gene Moore Blue.

The stakes in the windows game were high by the 1960s and 1970s in New York City, and the connection to the glamor and debauchery of the fashion scene at the time was strong. A series of big-name window designers were assigned to big stores, and while they all socialized and stayed out far too late, the competition to one-up one other was intense. Candy Pratts Price was hanging mannequins upside down at Bloomingdale's. Halston's boyfriend Victor Hugo was creating chaotic narratives in the windows of Halston's Madison Avenue shop. And Robert Currie was shocking passersby by putting housewives in lingerie, couture clothing surrounded by garbage, and a boudoir murder scene in the windows at Henri Bendel. They would put live people in windows or light cigarettes and leave them to let the smoke billow and waft. There were no laws and no restrictions. The imagination reigned supreme. But no one ever did it better than Gene Moore, who created nearly

Diamond engagement ring window, Fall, 2017. Photo © Ricky Zehavi.

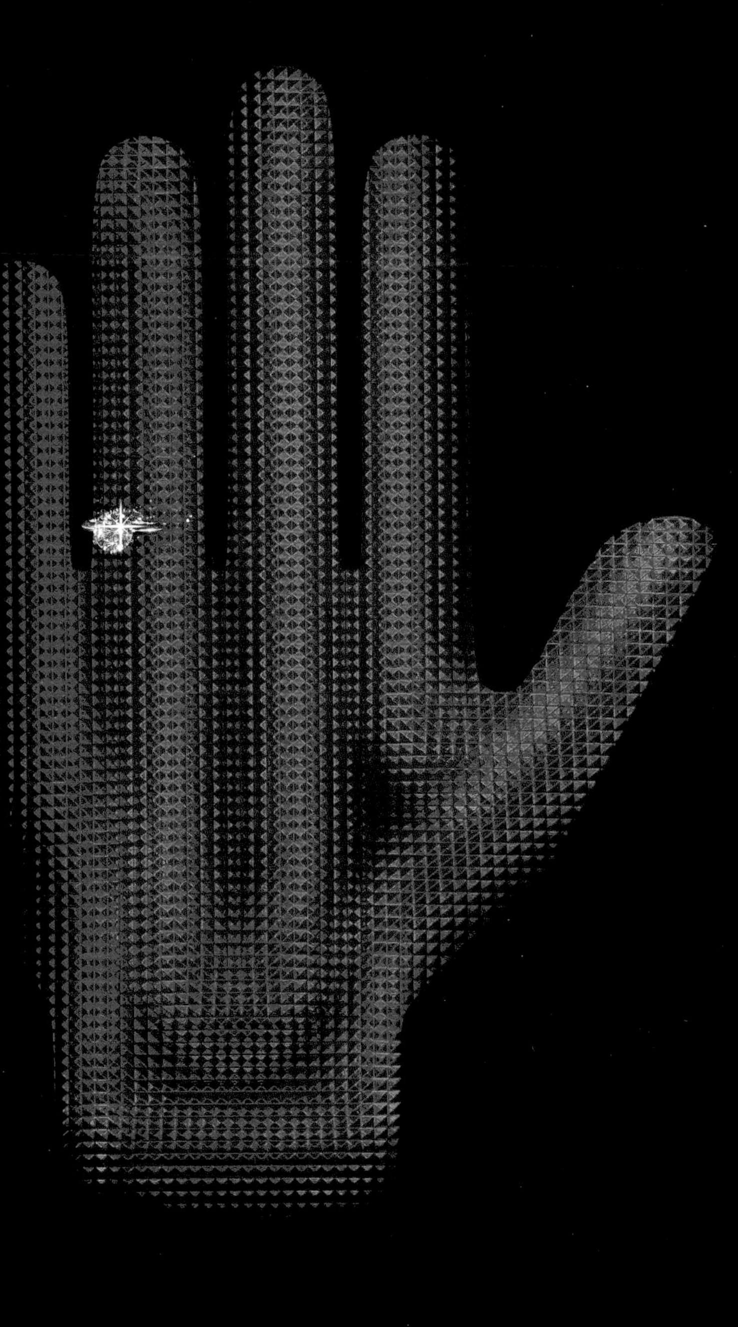

5,000 windows for Tiffany during his 39 years with the store. Couturière Pauline Trigère once said of Moore: "He could make a carrot glamorous."

Display has always been closely tied to fine art, and so it draws dreamers and artisans filled with ideas and searching for a forum for expression. In the intricate worlds inside a window, they can paint backdrops, create sculptures, draw, sketch, and experiment with lighting, all with a built-in audience and the relief of regular income. Gene Moore nurtured the talent of many great artists before they were anyone to know. In the mid 1950s, he hired Jasper Johns and Robert Rauschenberg, working under the pseudonym Matson Jones, to create windows with him. Rauschenberg once joked: "Moore noticed me before Leo Castelli did." And many New Yorkers first saw the work of Andy Warhol in the windows at Tiffany, long before he became the idiosyncratic father of the Pop Art movement.

The store window remains a potent outlet for creative expression, where the artistic spirit breathes and shines. But its function today is very different from the pedestrian street theater it once was. Windows today, just like everything else, live in service to social media. While 20 million people may walk past the Fifth Avenue flagship windows each year, the photographs they take and post on various social platforms amplify the reach of creativity exponentially, carrying the image of something that may have been carefully crafted by hand in a small workshop into corners of the world and to fresh eyes that Gene Moore could never have imagined. This extrapolation of image has changed how Tiffany's windows are designed, challenging everyone who works on them to consider their installation to insure that a three-dimensional space will still be eloquent and intriguing, even when rendered in a two-dimensional photograph. The desire remains to connect intimately with one's audience, even if that audience is now almost unimaginably vast.

Today, under the direction of Richard Moore (no relation to Gene Moore) and Christopher Young, Tiffany's window designs are visually worked out in advance, often hand-sketched or rendered in watercolor for creative approval. A large number of these designs are carefully housed in the legendary Tiffany archives, alongside nearly two centuries of Tiffany jewelry designs and objects from the company's enormous collection. Modern technology has expanded the creative possibilities for these renderings exponentially. LED and digitally controlled instruments allow for more precise lighting and a rich spectrum far beyond Gene Moore's colored lighting gels. Digital animation creates movement and life. Laser cutting machines allow for exacting detail and intricacy in even the smallest components of an installation. And, through 3D modeling and printing technology, designers are able to experiment with scaled or forced perspective, and even print a 3D model version of the entire window before it's installed for jewelry rigging and lighting purposes. What has not changed, however, is the vivid imagination of the people who create these windows. Many have illustration and set-design backgrounds, and are well versed in storytelling, architectural history, one-, two- and three-point perspective and color theory to bring tangible magic to their work. All of them are artists, each one a dreamer.

It is Tiffany & Co.'s great fortune to have the moment of amazement and longing while gazing into a shop window iconized in *Breakfast at Tiffany's.* In the film, Holly Golightly, played by Audrey Hepburn, says there is only one antidote when she is overcome by the feeling of the "mean reds," an edgier and more anxious version of the blues: "Well, when I get it the only thing that does any good is to jump in a cab and go to Tiffany's. Calms me down right away. The quietness and the proud look of it; nothing very bad could happen to you there." This golden moment of pop culture has helped insinuate into people's hearts and minds that there is wonder to be found at the corner of 57th Street and Fifth Avenue.

Inside these famous windows, art, sculpture, lighting, and set design come together to create a moment of pure beauty, perhaps all the more seductive for its fleeting nature. A window is the ultimate gallery, a compressed narrative that blends the rough with the polished, reality with illusion, purposefulness with imperfection, subtle humor with social commentary. Here desire may turn into need, or maybe just a pleasant daydream. Either way, every window is an invitation to believe in something a little bigger than oneself. But it is, always, a gracious invitation. In the words of Gene Moore: "Windows should be polite, because they talk to strangers."

Audrey Hepburn as Holly Golightly looking through the windows at the Tiffany and Co. flagship store in New York City in *Breakfast at Tiffany's*, 1961. Photo courtesy Bridgeman Images, reproduced with the permission of the Audrey Hepburn Estate.

Long
AMERICA

DISPLAY OTHER SIDE
FOR HOUSEKEEPING
DO NOT
DISTURB
TIFFANY & CO
925
NEW YORK
NY

TIFFANY & CO.
TIFFANY & CO.
NEW YORK
TIFFANY & CO
first
aid
TIFFANY & CO.

DELICIOUS
NUTRITIOUS
HEALTHFUL
APPETIZING

POP
CORN
DELICIOUS
NUTRITIOUS
HEALTHFUL
APPETIZING

Cravin' Rum Raisin
Tuttifrutti Fruttiloopi
Orange Kiss
Sassy Sassafrass
Diamond Dish Delish

Very Sparkleberry
Rococo Cocoa
Peridot Pistachio

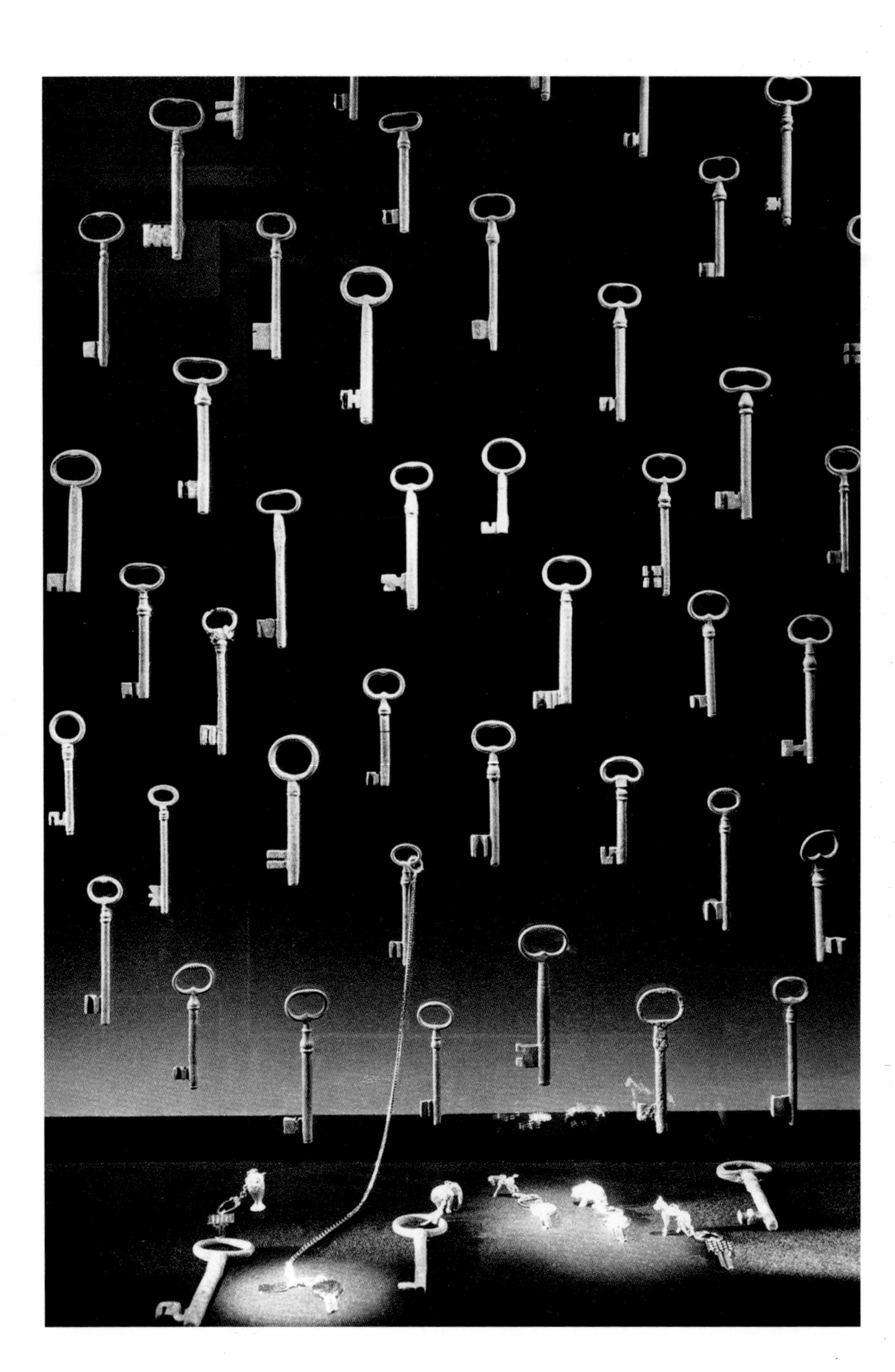

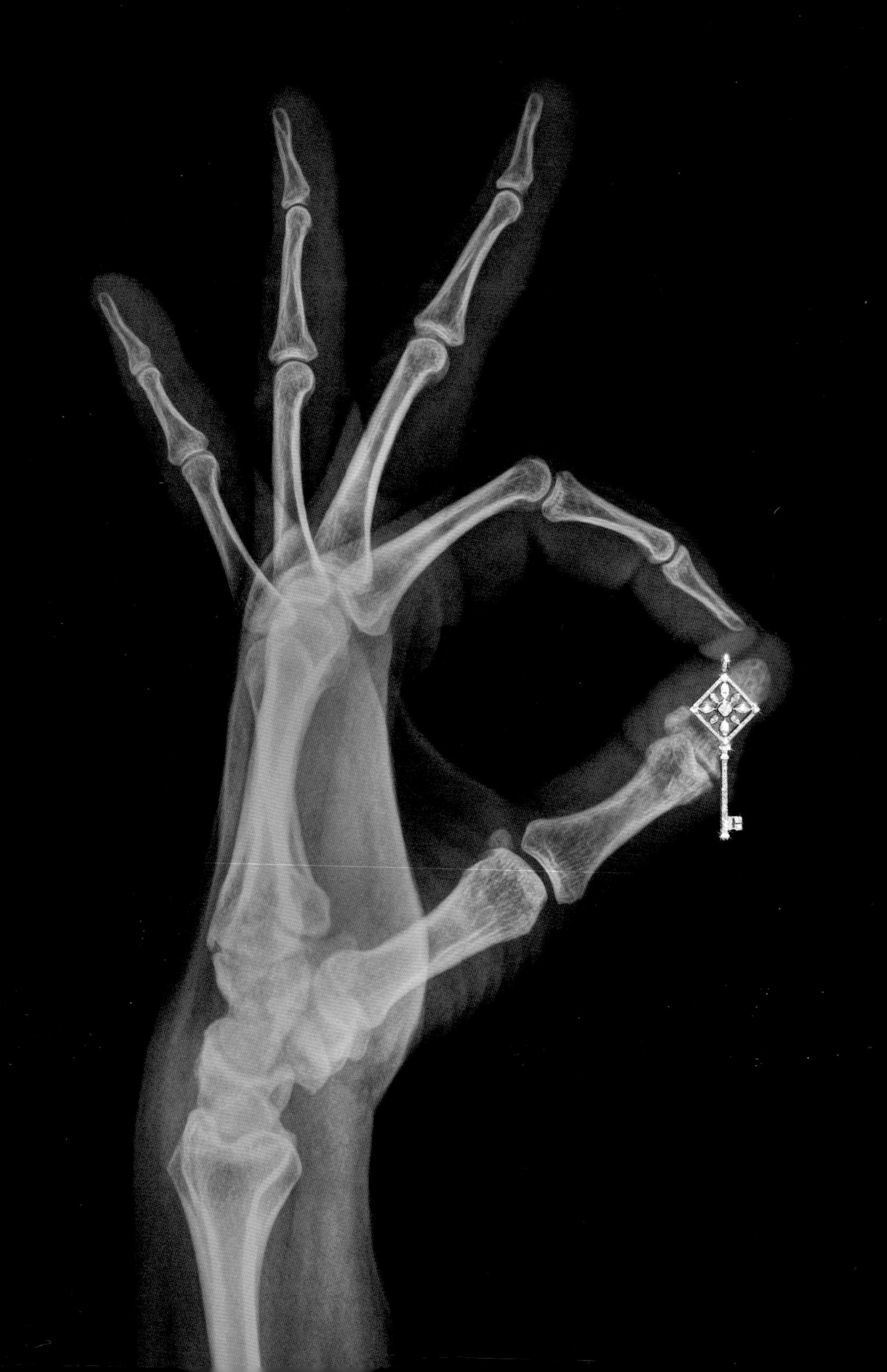

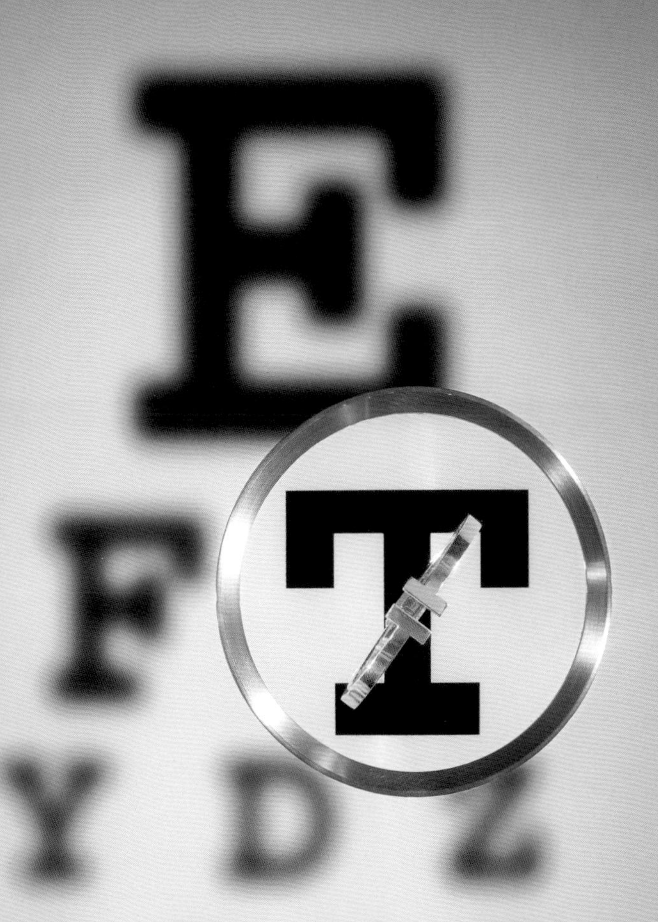

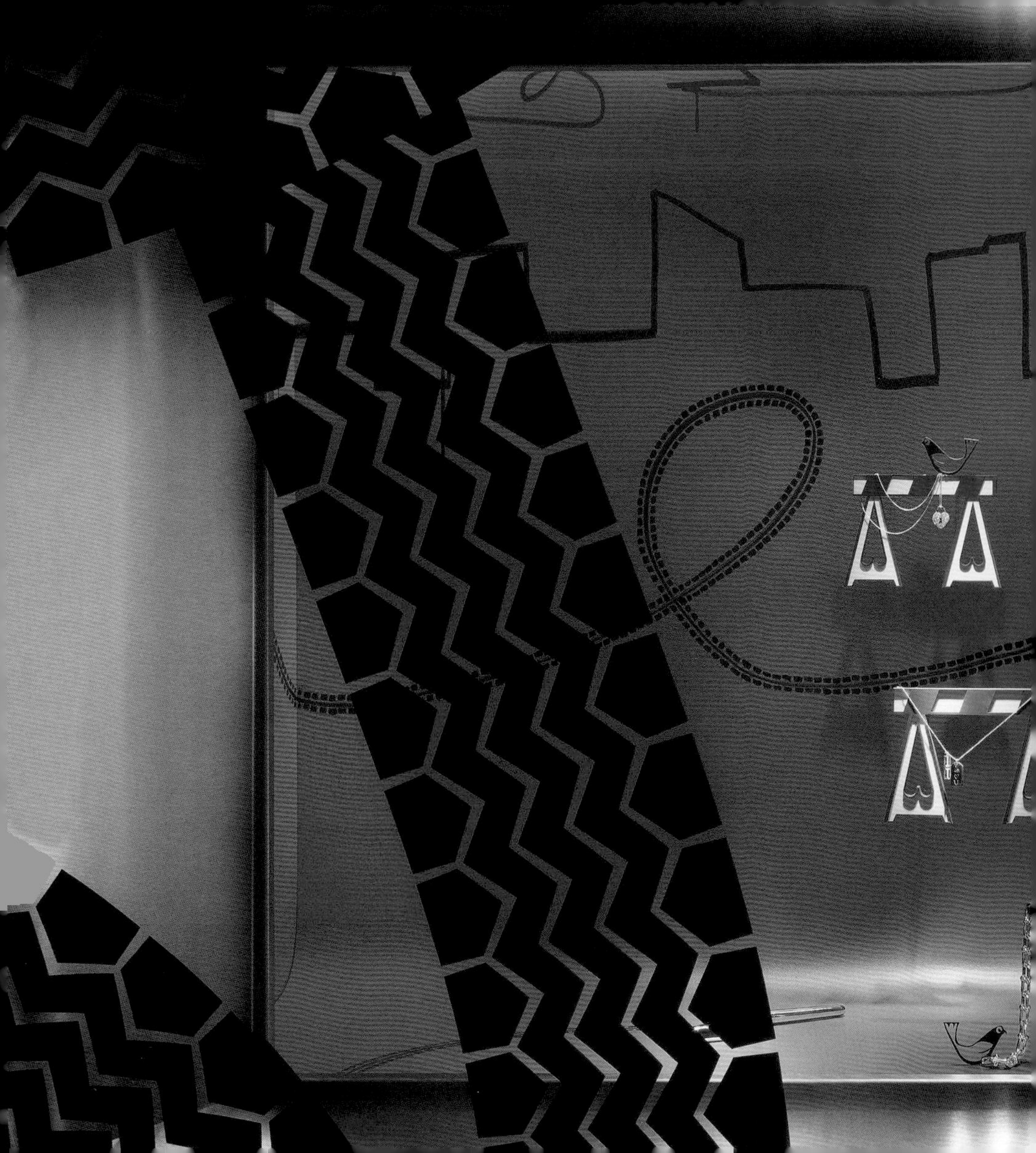

Mr. Williams &
Mr. Edwards
VALENTINES DAY EDITION

ST
5 AV

PLEASE RETURN TO
LOVE
TIFFANY&Co
NEW YORK

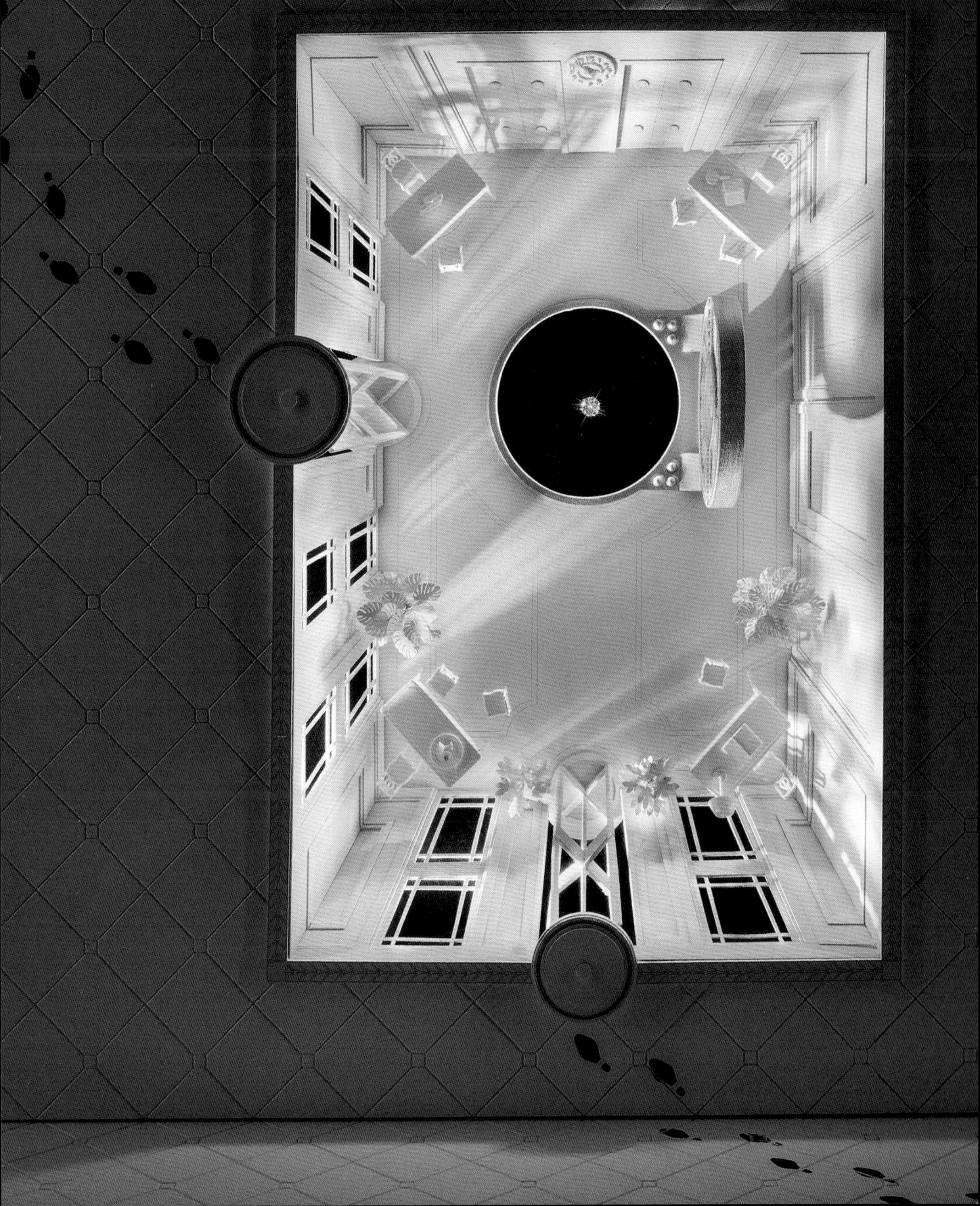

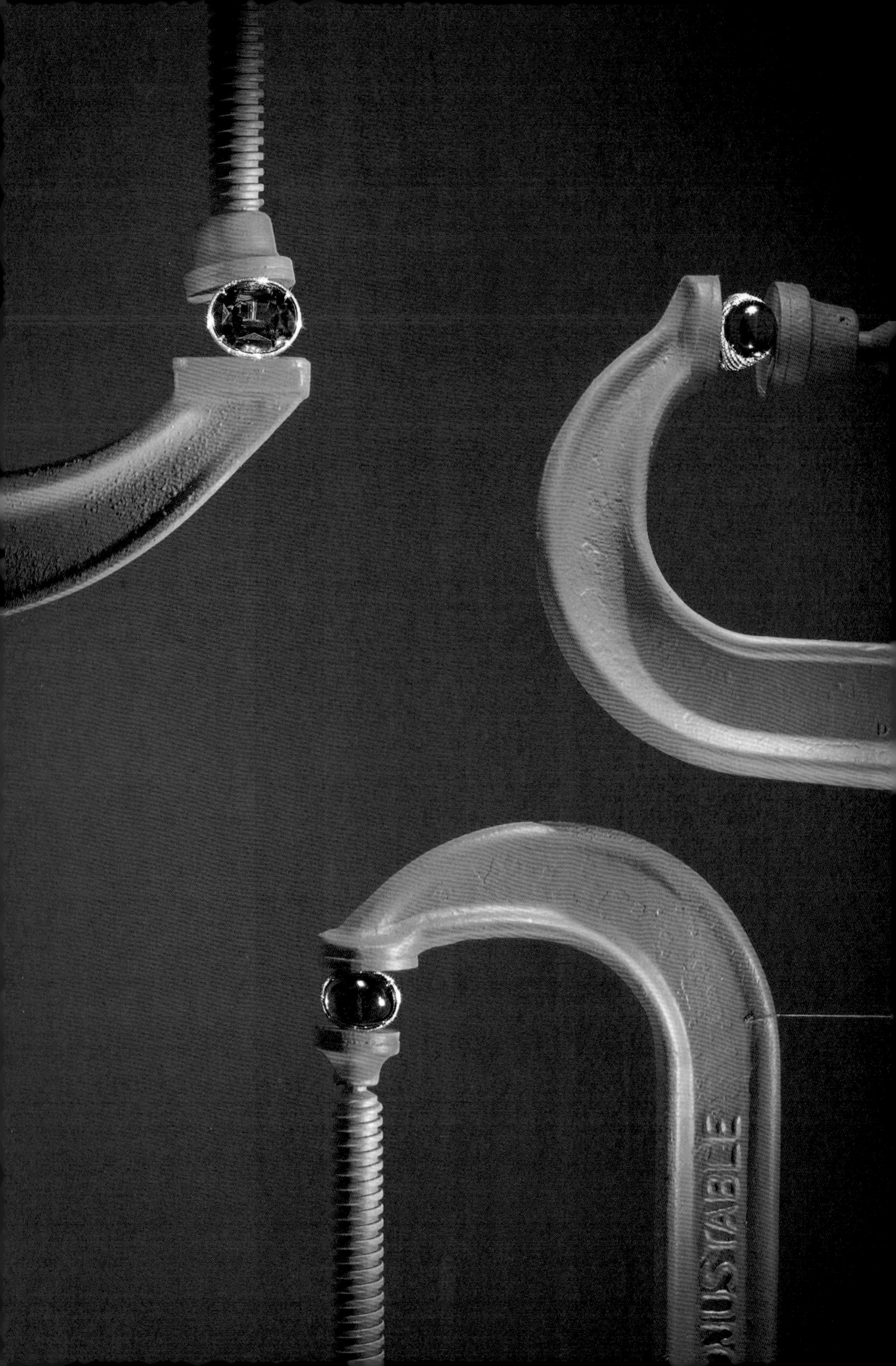

AMERICA'S BEST
Songbird
NO. 1837
NET WEIGHT
800 GRAMS
BIRD SEED
PACKED BY
INTERNATIONAL BIRD PRODUCTS LTD.
NEW YORK, NY

AMERICA'S BEST

BIRD FEEDERS
APPROVED
OF NEW YORK

5TH AVE
E. 57 ST
TIFFANY & CO.

ROAD TRIP
EPIK
2nd Anniversary
КОХАННЯ
Welcome 2018!
70s FUNK
DREAMS of BulGogi
Моє Серденько...
XOX♥XO 6/15
우리의 추억 (2012)
Our Songs Vol. I
ALTERNATIVE
SURF TUNES
BFF
ROCK
Я ТЕБЕ ЛЮБЛЮ
He loves me / He loves me not
BROOKLYN
PURE MAGIC
PUNK
HONEY
TIFFANY & CO.
LOVES ME
Loves Me
9·23·11
좋아하는 사람 너!
MUSIC
사랑♥사랑♥사랑
BIG CITY
-By ME
Heart Breaker
LETS MAKE A SPLASH!
For my Mister
Be KIND... REWIND!
MAKE OUT Mix
GLADWELL
DAC
120 MIN

FINALS
When Doves Cry
GLADWELL
BOOGIE!
DAC DIAMOND AUDIO CORPORATION
120 MIN.
XOXOXO
Queen Mix
JAZZ
我愛你
YO-YO MIX!!
METAL
BABE...
Love
You spin me
NYC BEATS
Secret Admirer
HIP HOP
MIX
for you
OLD SCHOOL
SPRING BREAK
¡esta bueno!
YASSSSSSS!
MEXICO City Mix
REMIX
flute
bisou bisou

LOVE
L
LOVE
Love
TIFFANY setting
SDR 1

L
V
E

WA
OPEN

Mr. Edwards
Nullam mollis eros et nisl condimentum
Vivamus sagittis nibh nec nibh finibus
Harris &
Bonalli

K This WAY

TIFFANY & CO.

Luminance
SUPRACOLOR

WINDOWS
at TIFFANY & CO.

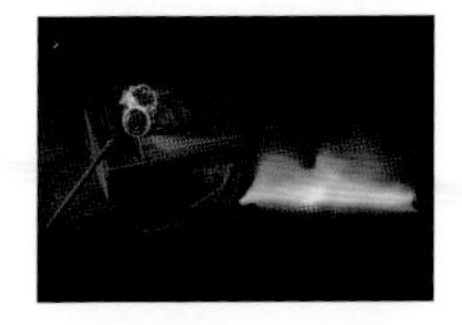

Fanning the Flames of Desire, high jewelry spessartine rings, 2017.
Photo: © Ricky Zehavi.

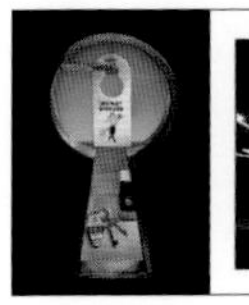

(I Do) Not Disturb, diamond ring engagement window, 2018.
Photo: © Ricky Zehavi.
Laws of Attraction, Modern Love campaign, 2018. Photo: © Ricky Zehavi.

Coney Island, candy apples and rubelite rings, 2017.
Photo: © Ricky Zehavi.

Coney Island, colored cocktail rings, 2017. Photo: © Ricky Zehavi.

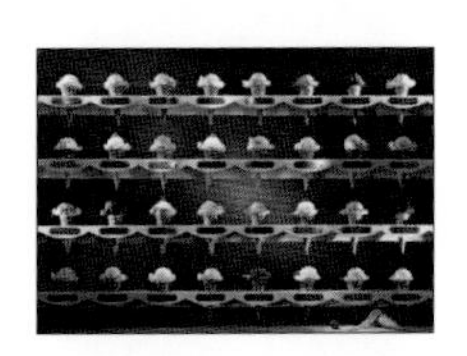

Ice Cream, colored cocktail rings, Summer series, 2011. Photo: © Ricky Zehavi.

Keys, Gene Moore, September 24, 1962. Photo: © Nick Malan Studio Inc.
Design for the *Vanderbilt Gate* window, celebrating the Central Park Conservancy, 2012. Watercolor: © Christopher Young.

What took you so long?!, Valentine's Day, 2017. Photo: © Ricky Zehavi.

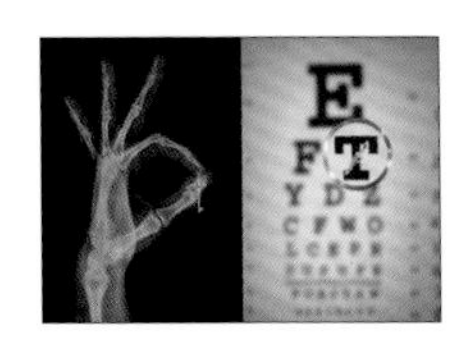

X-Ray, featuring the Tiffany Keys yellow diamond key, Fall, 2017.
Photo: © Ricky Zehavi.
Eye See Tiffany T, Fall, 2017. Photo: © Ricky Zehavi.

The Ice Carver, Holiday, 2017. This window features miniature crystal chandeliers made for Tiffany & Co. by Lobmeyr; exact replicas of the iconic Lobmeyr chandeliers at the Metropolitan Opera in New York City.
Photo: © Ricky Zehavi.

Cupid's Arrows, Valentine's Day, 2014. Photo: © Ricky Zehavi.
Did you Ring?, Valentine's Day, 2015. Photo: © Ricky Zehavi.

The Mousetrap with a significant yellow diamond ring, Spring, 2017.
Photo: © Ricky Zehavi.

Motorcycle, Valentine's Day, 2018. Photo: © Ricky Zehavi.

Traffic Cop, Valentine's Day, 2018. Photo: © Ricky Zehavi.
House of Tiffany, 2016. Photo: © Ricky Zehavi.

The House of Tiffany, 2016. Photo: © Ricky Zehavi.

Colored cocktail rings, Spring, 2017. Photo: © Ricky Zehavi.
Tiffany & Co. Schlumberger® amethyst Bird on a Rock with bird seed, Spring, 2017. Photo: © Ricky Zehavi.

Concept collage for Spring 2018. Photo: © Zeno Peduzzi.
Spring window, 2018. Photo: © Ricky Zehavi.

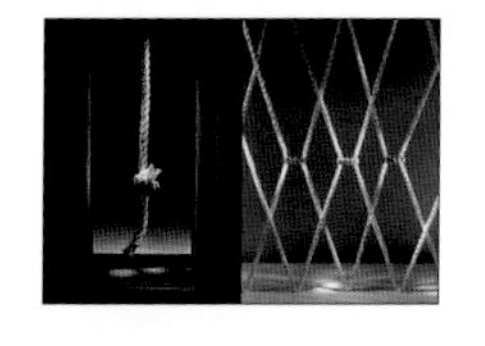

Butterfly, Gene Moore, February 15, 1972, photograph digitally colorized by Christopher Young. Photo: © Nick Malan Studio Inc. Photography.
Crossing Ropes, Gene Moore, 1970, photograph digitally colorized by Christopher Young. Photo: © Nick Malan Studio Inc. Photography.

Love Notes, 2018. Photo: © Ricky Zehavi.

Illustration design for *Holiday, 2015,* watercolor and white gouache on toned paper. Photo: © Christopher Young.
Holiday, 2015. Photo: © Ricky Zehavi.

A Diamond Iceberg, Holiday, 2016. Truman Capote once described Manhattan as "A diamond iceberg floating in river water," and this window pays homage to the glamour and the majesty of New York City. Photo: © Ricky Zehavi.
Tiffany High Impact, Fall, 2017. Photo: © Ricky Zehavi.

An Important diamond jewelry window, Spring, 2017. Photo: © Ricky Zehavi.

4th of July, 2013. Photo: © Ricky Zehavi.

Concept sketches for Valentine's Day, 2015. © Christopher Young.
Box of Chocolates, Valentine's Day, 2015. Photo: © Ricky Zehavi.

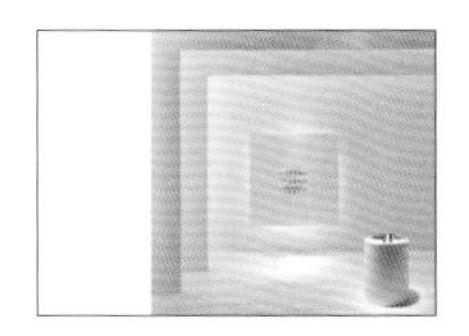

Tiffany T Gallery window, Fall 2014. Photo: © Ricky Zehavi.

Dogwalker, Valentine's Day, 2018. Photo: © Ricky Zehavi.

The Great Gatsby window collaboration with Baz Luhrmann and Academy Award winner Catherine Martin, jewels featured were worn in the major motion picture, Spring, 2013. Photo: © Ricky Zehavi.
Tiffany Blue Book window, Fall, 2011. Photo: © Ricky Zehavi.

Schlumberger at Coney Island, 2017. Photo: © Ricky Zehavi.

The Winter Picnic, Design for Holiday window, 2016.
Photo: © Christopher Young.
Make the World Sparkle, Holiday, 2016. Photo: © Ricky Zehavi.

The Winter Picnic, Holiday 2016. Photo: © Ricky Zehavi.

Work in progress. Behind the scenes of the Tiffany windows.
All photos: © Dan Wonderly, except far left center: © Mary Frances Flournoy.

Holiday facade, 2017. Photo: © Ricky Zehavi.

Acknowledgments

With respect and gratitude to:

Adam Shehab, Alessandro Arensberg, Alessandro Bogliolo, Ali Kashfi, Anders Olson, Anna Harrow, Arnulfo Maldonado, Arthur Shramko, Aviva Stanoff Designs, Baz Luhrmann, Benson Knight, BeSide Digital, Brian Bustos, Brian Kalin, Burke & Pryde, Caroline Naggiar, Catherine Martin, Cheh Jiwoong, Chisato Uno, Christine Caponi, Christopher Young, Codec, Coeur Noir, Colbar Art, Cory Barrett, Cosmopolitan Glass, Dan Wonderly, Definite Films, Doss Freel, Duggal, Emily Lin, Emma Morgan, Erik Grathwohl, Eunice Bae, Form & Space, Frederic Cumenal, Isabel Von Fluegge, Jake Messing, Jason Lajka, Jay Sydow, Karen Silveira, Kerry Feldmann, Kimie Nishikawa, Kris Lang, Kristie Huey, Lab Partners, Laura Myslinsky, Linda Nastaszewski, Lite Brite Neon Studio, Lobmeyr, Lowell Detweiler, Lucy-Ann Bouwman, Lux Haac, Mary Frances Flournoy, Max Wittert, Melanie Summers, Michael C. DiPrato, Michael J. Kowalski, Michael Krynski, Millennium Signs & Display, Nabil Samadani, Nicole Colomara, Pacific Northern, Pam Cloud, Paul Han, Phantom Limb, Phillip Tokarsky, Porzellanmanufaktur Nymphenburg, Rachel Zoe, Reed Krakoff, Richard Moore, Ricky Zehavi, Robert Henderson, Robert Sorrell, Rubelli, Ryan Becker, Sculpture House Casting, Sean Robertson, Shane Ruth, Simon Cleveland, Space-Craft Worldwide, Spaeth Design, Stephan Moravski, Tella Friedewald, The Green Vase, Two Seven, Tyler Flatt, Vivienne Bell, Wanglong, and YESCO.

Assouline publishing would like to thank Michael Luther, Thomas Haggerty, Bridgeman Images, and Michael O. Crain, Crain Law Group, LLC on behalf of Sean Hepburn Ferrer.

PRISMACOLOR | PREMIER
SUPRACOLOR II Soft
CARAN d'ACHE · SWISS MADE
Luminance 6901
KOBALTGRÜN COBALT GREEN
VERT TURQUOISE · TURQUOISE GREEN
AQUAMARINE
AIGUE-MARINE
Albrecht Dürer
FABER-CASTELL
KOBALTTÜRKIS HELL LIGHT COBALT TURQUOISE
BLEU TURQUOISE · TURQUOISE